Where does the Squirrel Sleep?

Grant Dawson

ILLUSTRATIONS BY
Nathan Stromberg

red pine
PRESS

For my wife, whom I adore.

- Grant Dawson

For June, Greta and Ben. I love you, now go to sleep.

- Nathan Stromberg

Layout by Shalanah Dawson

Printed in the United States of America.

RedPinePress.com
First Edition, 2017

ISBN 978-0-9990121-0-9

red pine PRESS

To all tender children with nodding heads,
who ponder about other animals' beds.

Where does the squirrel sleep?

The squirrel snuggles in for a nighttime rest,
high on a branch in her own leafy nest.

Where does the robin sleep?

He's dreaming of earthworms up in his perch,
in a thimble of grass on the branch of a birch.

ome where
mother had
Bergmann, a
like
been taken
asked in finding
large part of her

Where does the otter sleep?

Cuddled together, for safety it seems,

adrift on the tranquil ocean of dreams.

Where does the frog sleep?

As still as a stone, hidden in the reeds,

a pocket of damp is all that it needs.

Where does the falcon sleep?

On a windblown craggy cliffside she clings,

with her head buried under saffron wings.

Where does the bee sleep?

Their papery orb is the inn that they keep,

when they are done making honey, they sleep.

Where does the deer sleep?

She swirls amber grasses into a bed,

then she gathers her hooves, and lays her head.

Where does the beaver sleep?

At noon, in a lodge, he's unconcerned, slumbering,
because all night before he was arduously lumbering.

Where does the lion sleep?

On the savannah, with nothing to hide,

he dozes while safely guarding his pride.

Where does the fox sleep?

In the quiet corner of a shaded dale,
curled in close under a blanket of tail.

Sleep, little children, like these creatures do.
If you dream of them, maybe they'll dream of you.

About the Author

Grant Dawson lives with his wife and cat in Saint Paul, MN. He loves fishing, reading, songwriting and going on very long walks. This is his first book for children.

About the Illustrator

Nathan Stromberg lives with his wife and three children in Saint Paul, where squirrels often doze outside of his kitchen window. He teaches art to high school students across the river in Minneapolis and exhibits his art regionally and nationally. You can see his artwork at nathanstromberg.com

Love the book?

You can find us at

WhereDoesTheSquirrelSleep.com

Order another copy,
send one as a gift,
or order a print of your
favorite piece of artwork.

Now, hush!
Lights out!

red pine
PRESS